THE
LITTLE BOOK OF
SELF-CARE
— FOR —
SAGITTARIUS

Simple Ways to Refresh and Restore—According to the Stars

CONSTANCE STELLAS

ADAMS MEDIA

NEW YORK LONDON TORONTO SYDNEY NEW DELHI

Adamsmedia

Adams Media
An Imprint of Simon & Schuster, Inc.
100 Technology Center Drive
Stoughton, MA 02072

First Adams Media hardcover edition January 2019

ADAMS MEDIA and colophon are trademarks of Simon & Schuster.

For information about special discounts for bulk purchases,
please contact Simon & Schuster Special Sales at 1-866-506-1949 or business@simonandschuster.com.

The Simon & Schuster Speakers Bureau can bring authors to your live event. For more information or to book an event contact the Simon & Schuster Speakers Bureau at 1-866-248-3049 or visit our website at www.simonspeakers.com.

Interior design by Colleen Cunningham
Interior images © Getty Images; Clipart.com

Manufactured in China
10 9 8 7

Library of Congress Cataloging-in-Publication Data
Names: Stellas, Constance, author.
Title: The little book of self-care for Sagittarius / Constance Stellas.
Description: Avon, Massachusetts: Adams Media, 2019.
Series: Astrology self-care.
Identifiers: LCCN 2018038265 |

ISBN 9781507209806 (hc) | ISBN 9781507209813 (ebook)
Subjects: LCSH: Sagittarius (Astrology) | Self-care, Health--Miscellanea.
Classification: LCC BF1727.6 .S74 2019 | DDC 133.5/274--dc23
LC record available at https://lccn.loc.gov/2018038265

ISBN 978-1-5072-0980-6
ISBN 978-1-5072-0981-3 (ebook)

Dedication

To my wandering and searching
Sagittarian friends and clients.

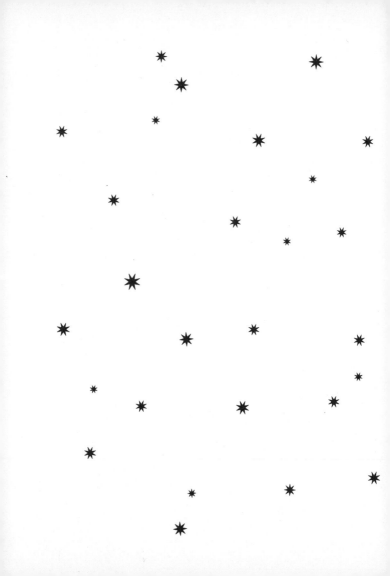

CONTENTS

Acknowledgments

I would like to thank Karen Cooper and everyone at Adams Media who helped with this book. To Brendan O'Neill, Katie Corcoran Lytle, Sarah Doughty, Eileen Mullan, Casey Ebert, Sylvia Davis, and everyone else who worked on the manuscripts. To Frank Rivera, Colleen Cunningham, and Katrina Machado for their work on the book's cover and interior design. I appreciated your team spirit and eagerness to dive into the riches of astrology.

Introduction

It's time for you to have a little *"me"* time—powered by the zodiac. By tapping into your Sun sign's astrological and elemental energies, *The Little Book of Self-Care for Sagittarius* brings star-powered strength and cosmic relief to your life with self-care guidance tailored specifically for you.

While you may enjoy being constantly on the go, Sagittarius, this book focuses on your true self. This book provides information on how to incorporate self-care into your life while teaching you just how important astrology is to your overall self-care routine. You'll learn more about yourself as you learn about your sign and its governing element, fire. Then you can relax, rejuvenate, and stay balanced with more than one hundred self-care ideas and activities perfect for your Sagittarius personality.

From watching a funny film to meditating near water, you will find plenty of ways to heal your mind, body, and active spirit. Now, let the stars be your self-care guide!

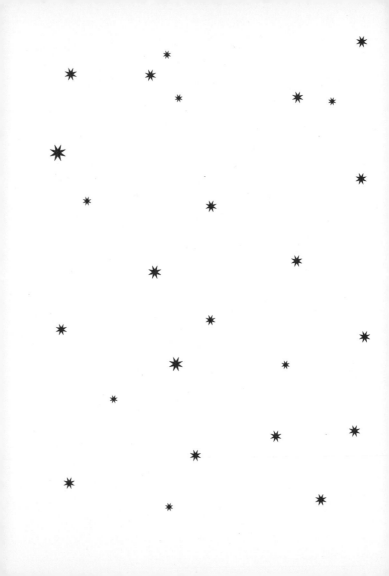

PART 1

SIGNS, ELEMENTS, ___ AND ___ SELF-CARE

CHAPTER 1
WHAT IS SELF-CARE?

✳

Astrology gives insights into whom to love, when to charge forward into new beginnings, and how to succeed in whatever you put your mind to. When paired with self-care, astrology can also help you relax and reclaim that part of yourself that tends to get lost in the bustle of the day. In this chapter you'll learn what self-care is—for you. (No matter your sign, self-care is more than just lit candles and quiet reflection, though these activities may certainly help you find the renewal that you seek.) You'll also learn how making a priority of personalized self-care activities can benefit you in ways you may not even have thought of. Whether you're a Leo, a Pisces, or a Taurus, you deserve rejuvenation and renewal that's customized to your sign—this chapter reveals where to begin.

What Self-Care Is

Self-care is any activity that you do to take care of yourself. It rejuvenates your body, refreshes your mind, or realigns your spirit. It relaxes and refuels you. It gets you ready for a new day or a fresh start. It's the practices, rituals, and meaningful activities that you do, just for you, that help you feel safe, grounded, happy, and fulfilled.

The activities that qualify as self-care are amazingly unique and personalized to who you are, what you like, and, in large part, what your astrological sign is. If you're asking questions about what self-care practices are best for those ruled by fire and born under Sagittarius, you'll find answers—and restoration—in Part 2. But, no matter which of those self-care activities speak to you and your unique place in the universe on any given day, it will fall into one of the following self-care categories—each of which pertains to a different aspect of your life:

* Physical self-care
* Emotional self-care
* Social self-care
* Mental self-care
* Spiritual self-care
* Practical self-care

When you practice all of these unique types of self-care—and prioritize your practice to ensure you are choosing the best options for your unique sign and governing element—know that you are actively working to create the version of yourself that the universe intends you to be.

Physical Self-Care

When you practice physical self-care, you make the decision to look after and restore the one physical body that has been bestowed upon you. Care for it. Use it in the best way you can imagine, for that is what the universe wishes you to do. You can't light the world on fire or move mountains if you're not doing everything you can to take care of your physical health.

Emotional Self-Care

Emotional self-care is when you take the time to acknowledge and care for your inner self, your emotional well-being. Whether you're angry or frustrated, happy or joyful, or somewhere in between, emotional self-care happens when you choose to sit with your emotions: when you step away from the noise of daily life that often drowns out or tamps down your authentic self. Emotional self-care lets you see your inner you as the cosmos intend. Once you identify your true emotions, you can either accept them and continue to move forward on your journey or you can try to change any negative emotions for the better. The more you acknowledge your feelings and practice emotional self-care, the more you'll feel the positivity that the universe and your life holds for you.

Social Self-Care

You practice social self-care when you nurture your relationships with others, be they friends, coworkers, or family members. In today's hectic world it's easy to let relationships fall to the wayside, but it's so important to share your life with others—and let others share their lives with you. Social self-care is reciprocal and often karmic. The support and love that you put out into the universe through social self-care is given back to you by those you socialize with—often tenfold.

Mental Self-Care

Mental self-care is anything that keeps your mind working quickly and critically. It helps you cut through the fog of the day, week, or year and ensures that your quick wit and sharp mind are intact and working the way the cosmos intended. Making sure your mind is fit helps you problem-solve, decreases stress since you're not feeling overwhelmed, and keeps you feeling on top of your mental game—no matter your sign or your situation.

Spiritual Self-Care

Spiritual self-care is self-care that allows you to tap into your soul and the soul of the universe and uncover its secrets. Rather than focusing on a particular religion or set of religious beliefs, these types of self-care activities reconnect you with a higher power: the sense that something out there is bigger than you. When you meditate, you connect. When you pray, you connect. Whenever you do something that allows you to experience and marry yourself to the vastness that is the cosmos, you practice spiritual self-care.

Practical Self-Care

Self-care is what you do to take care of yourself, and practical self-care, while not as expansive as the other types, is made up of the seemingly small day-to-day tasks that bring you peace and accomplishment. These practical self-care rituals are important, but are often overlooked. Scheduling a doctor's appointment that you've been putting off is practical self-care. Getting your hair cut is practical self-care. Anything you can check off your list of things to be accomplished gives you a sacred space to breathe and allows the universe more room to bring a beautiful sense of cosmic fulfillment your way.

What Self-Care Isn't

Self-care is restorative. Self-care is clarifying. Self-care is whatever you need to do to make yourself feel secure in the universe.

Now that you know what self-care is, it's also important that you're able to see what self-care isn't. Self-care is not something that you force yourself to do because you think it will be good for you. Some signs are energy in motion and sitting still goes against their place in the universe. Those signs won't feel refreshed by lying in a hammock or sitting down to meditate. Other signs aren't able to ground themselves unless they've found a self-care practice that protects their cosmic need for peace and quiet. Those signs won't find parties, concerts, and loud venues soothing or satisfying. If a certain ritual doesn't bring you peace, clarity, or satisfaction, then it's not right for your sign and you should find something that speaks to you more clearly.

There's a difference though between not finding satisfaction in a ritual that you've tried and not wanting to try a self-care activity because you're tired or stuck in a comfort zone. Sometimes going to the gym or meeting up with friends is the self-care practice that you need to experience—whether engaging in it feels like a downer or not. So consider how you feel when you're actually doing the activity. If it feels invigorating to get on the treadmill or you feel delight when you actually catch up with your friend, the ritual is doing what it should be doing and clearing space for you—among other benefits...

The Benefits of Self-Care

The benefits of self-care are boundless and there's none that's superior to helping you put rituals in place to feel more at home in your body, in your spirit, and in your unique home in the cosmos. There are, however, other benefits to engaging in the practice of self-care that you should know.

Rejuvenates Your Immune System

No matter which rituals are designated for you by the stars, your sign, and its governing element, self-care helps both your body and mind rest, relax, and recuperate. The practice of self-care activates the parasympathetic nervous system (often called the rest and digest system), which slows your heart rate, calms the body, and overall helps your body relax and release tension. This act of decompression gives your body the space it needs to build up and strengthen your immune system, which protects you from illness.

Helps You Reconnect—with Yourself

When you practice the ritual of self-care—especially when you customize this practice based on your personal sign and governing element—you learn what you like to do and what you need to do to replenish yourself. Knowing yourself better, and allowing yourself the time and space that you need to focus on your personal needs and desires, gives you the gifts of self-confidence and self-knowledge. Setting time aside to focus on your needs also helps you put busy, must-do things aside, which gives you time to reconnect with yourself and who you are deep inside.

Increases Compassion

Perhaps one of the most important benefits of creating a self-care ritual is that, by focusing on yourself, you become more compassionate to others as well. When you truly take the time to care for yourself and make yourself and your importance in the universe a priority in your own life, you're then able to care for others and see their needs and desires in a new way. You can't pour from an empty dipper, and self-care allows you the space and clarity to do what you can to send compassion out into the world.

Starting a Self-Care Routine

Self-care should be treated as a ritual in your life, something you make the time to pause for, no matter what. You are important. You deserve rejuvenation and a sense of relaxation. You need to open your soul to the gifts that the universe is giving you, and self-care provides you with a way to ensure you're ready to receive those gifts. To begin a self-care routine, start by making yourself the priority. Do the customized rituals in Part 2 with intention, knowing the universe has already given them to you, by virtue of your sign and your governing element.

Now that you understand the role that self-care will hold in your life, let's take a closer look at the connection between self-care and astrology.

CHAPTER 2

SELF-CARE
AND ASTROLOGY

✳

Astrology is the study of the connection between the objects in the heavens (the planets, the stars) and what happens here on earth. Just as the movements of the planets and other heavenly bodies influence the ebb and flow of the tides, so do they influence you—your body, your mind, your spirit. This relationship is ever present and is never more important—or personal—than when viewed through the lens of self-care.

In this chapter you'll learn how the locations of these celestial bodies at the time of your birth affect you and define the self-care activities that will speak directly to you as a Leo, an Aries, a Capricorn, or any of the other zodiac signs. You'll see how the zodiac influences every part of your being and why ignoring its lessons can leave you feeling frustrated and unfulfilled. You'll also realize that, when you perform the rituals of self-care based on your sign, the wisdom of the cosmos will lead you down a path of fulfillment and restoration—to the return of who you really are, deep inside.

Zodiac Polarities

In astrology, all signs are mirrored by other signs that are on the opposite side of the zodiac. This polarity ensures that the zodiac is balanced and continues to flow with an unbreakable, even stream of energy. There are two different polarities in the zodiac and each is called by a number of different names:

* Yang/masculine/positive polarity
* Yin/feminine/negative polarity

Each polar opposite embodies a number of opposing traits, qualities, and attributes that will influence which self-care practices will work for or against your sign and your own personal sense of cosmic balance.

Yang

Whether male or female, those who fall under yang, or masculine, signs are extroverted and radiate their energy outward. They are spontaneous, active, bold, and fearless. They move forward in life with the desire to enjoy everything the world has to offer to them, and they work hard to transfer their inspiration and positivity to others so that those individuals may experience the same gifts that the universe offers them. All signs governed by the fire and air elements are yang and hold the potential for these dominant qualities. We will refer to them with masculine pronouns. These signs are:

* Aries
* Leo
* Sagittarius
* Gemini
* Libra
* Aquarius

There are people who hold yang energy who are introverted and retiring. However, by practicing self-care that is customized for your sign and understanding the potential ways to use your energy, you can find a way—perhaps one that's unique to you—to claim your native buoyancy and dominance and engage with the path that the universe opens for you.

Yin

Whether male or female, those who fall under yin, or feminine, signs are introverted and radiate inwardly. They draw people and experiences to them rather than seeking people and experiences in an extroverted way. They move forward in life with an energy that is reflective, receptive, and focused on communication and achieving shared goals. All signs governed by the earth and water elements are yin and hold the potential for these reflective qualities. We will refer to them with feminine pronouns. These signs are:

* Taurus
* Virgo
* Capricorn
* Cancer
* Scorpio
* Pisces

As there are people with yang energy who are introverted and retiring, there are also people with yin energy who are outgoing and extroverted. And by practicing self-care rituals that speak to your particular sign, energy, and governing body, you will reveal your true self and the balance of energy will be maintained.

Governing Elements

Each astrological sign has a governing element that defines their energy orientation and influences both the way the sign moves through the universe and relates to self-care. The elements are fire, earth, air, and water. All the signs in each element share certain characteristics, along with having their own sign-specific qualities:

* **Fire:** Fire signs are adventurous, bold, and energetic. They enjoy the heat and warm environments and look to the sun and fire as a means to recharge their depleted batteries. They're competitive, outgoing, and passionate. The fire signs are Aries, Leo, and Sagittarius.
* **Earth:** Earth signs all share a common love and tendency toward a practical, material, sensual, and economic orientation. The earth signs are Taurus, Virgo, and Capricorn.
* **Air:** Air is the most ephemeral element and those born under this element are thinkers, innovators, and communicators. The air signs are Gemini, Libra, and Aquarius.
* **Water:** Water signs are instinctual, compassionate, sensitive, and emotional. The water signs are Cancer, Scorpio, and Pisces.

Chapter 3 teaches you all about the ways your specific governing element influences and drives your connection to your cosmically harmonious self-care rituals, but it's important that you realize how important these elemental traits are to your self-care practice and to the activities that will help restore and reveal your true self.

Sign Qualities

Each of the astrological elements governs three signs. Each of these three signs is also given its own quality or mode, which corresponds to a different part of each season: the beginning, the middle, or the end.

* **Cardinal signs:** The cardinal signs initiate and lead in each season. Like something that is just starting out, they are actionable, enterprising, and assertive, and are born leaders. The cardinal signs are Aries, Cancer, Libra, and Capricorn.
* **Fixed signs:** The fixed signs come into play when the season is well established. They are definite, consistent, reliable, motivated by principles, and powerfully stubborn. The fixed signs are Taurus, Leo, Scorpio, and Aquarius.
* **Mutable signs:** The mutable signs come to the forefront when the seasons are changing. They are part of one season, but also part of the next. They are adaptable, versatile, and flexible. The mutable signs are Gemini, Virgo, Sagittarius, and Pisces.

Each of these qualities tells you a lot about yourself and who you are. They also give you invaluable information about the types of self-care rituals that your sign will find the most intuitive and helpful.

Ruling Planets

In addition to qualities and elements, each specific sign is ruled by a particular planet that lends its personality to those born under that sign. Again, these sign-specific traits give you valuable insight into the personality of the signs and the self-care rituals that may best rejuvenate them. The signs that correspond to each planet—and the ways that those planetary influences determine your self-care options—are as follows:

* **Aries:** Ruled by Mars, Aries is passionate, energetic, and determined.
* **Taurus:** Ruled by Venus, Taurus is sensual, romantic, and fertile.
* **Gemini:** Ruled by Mercury, Gemini is intellectual, changeable, and talkative.
* **Cancer:** Ruled by the Moon, Cancer is nostalgic, emotional, and home loving.
* **Leo:** Ruled by the Sun, Leo is fiery, dramatic, and confident.
* **Virgo:** Ruled by Mercury, Virgo is intellectual, analytical, and responsive.
* **Libra:** Ruled by Venus, Libra is beautiful, romantic, and graceful.
* **Scorpio:** Ruled by Mars and Pluto, Scorpio is intense, powerful, and magnetic.
* **Sagittarius:** Ruled by Jupiter, Sagittarius is optimistic, boundless, and larger than life.

* **Capricorn:** Ruled by Saturn, Capricorn is wise, patient, and disciplined.
* **Aquarius:** Ruled by Uranus, Aquarius is independent, unique, and eccentric.
* **Pisces:** Ruled by Neptune and Jupiter, Pisces is dreamy, sympathetic, and idealistic.

A Word on Sun Signs

When someone is a Leo, Aries, Sagittarius, or any of the other zodiac signs, it means that the sun was positioned in this constellation in the heavens when they were born. Your Sun sign is a dominant factor in defining your personality, your best self-care practices, and your soul nature. Every person also has the position of the Moon, Mercury, Venus, Mars, Jupiter, Saturn, Uranus, Neptune, and Pluto. These planets can be in any of the elements: fire signs, earth signs, air signs, or water signs. If you have your entire chart calculated by an astrologer or on an Internet site, you can see the whole picture and learn about all your elements. Someone born under Leo with many signs in another element will not be as concentrated in the fire element as someone with five or six planets in Leo. Someone born in Pisces with many signs in another element will not be as concentrated in the water element as someone with five or six planets in Pisces. And so on. Astrology is a complex system and has many shades of meaning. For our purposes looking at the self-care practices designated by your Sun sign, or what most people consider their sign, will give you the information you need to move forward and find fulfillment and restoration.

ESSENTIAL ELEMENTS: FIRE

✳

Fire gives us heat, warmth, and light. And those who have fire as their governing element—like you, Sagittarius, as well as Aries and Leo—all have a special energy signature and connection with fire that guides all aspects of their lives. Fire signs are drawn to the flames in all its varied forms and environments whether this gift comes from the sun, an outdoor campfire, or a cozy fireplace fire, and their approach to self-care reflects their relationship with this fiery element. Let's take a look at the mythological importance of the sun, as well as the basic characteristics of the three fire signs, and what they all have in common when it comes to self-care.

The Mythology of Fire

In astrology, fire is considered the first element of creation. Perhaps it was primitive man's way of understanding the big bang, or maybe fire just made a clear-cut difference between living in the wild and gathering together in human communities. In Greek mythology the immortal Prometheus angered the gods by stealing fire for the mortals he had such affection for down on earth. As punishment he was chained to a rock and Zeus sent an eagle to eat his liver. Magically, this liver regenerated every day and the eagle kept devouring it. Prometheus was later released from this curse, but the gift of fire that he gave to mankind was not completely free of conflict.

Fire was—and remains—an essential part of civilized life, but it also gives humans the ability to forge weapons of war. Fire warms a home, cooks a meal, and restores and enlivens the spirit, but too much fire can destroy. All fire signs feel this duality between the creative and destructive force of their fire power energy, and this duality drives their likes and dislikes, personality traits, and approaches to self-care.

The Element of Fire

The fire signs are known as the inspirational signs because their enthusiasm and buoyant personalities help them to cheer themselves and others on to great success. They also represent the spiritual side of human nature and their sense of intuition is strong; fire signs often have hunches about themselves and others, and if they follow these hunches, they typically achieve whatever they set out to do. For example, Aries inspires the spark that pioneers a project or endeavor. Leo is a leader who inspires his circle of friends, family, or colleagues to keep their eyes on the goal at hand, even when things get tough. And Sagittarius is an idealist and searches (and helps others search) for truth.

Astrological Symbols

The astrological symbols (also called the zodiacal symbols) of the fire signs also give you hints as to how the fire signs move through the world. All of the fire signs are represented by animals of power and determination, which ties right back to their shared fiery element:

* Aries is the Ram
* Leo is the Lion
* Sagittarius is the Centaur (half horse/half man)

Each fire sign's personality and subsequent approaches to self-care connect to the qualities of these representative animals. For example, the Ram is determined and confident. The Lion is king of the jungle and boldly defends his turf. And the Centaur, also called the Archer, shoots his arrows of truth and moves powerfully against any attempts to rein him in.

Signs and Seasonal Modes

Each of the elements in astrology has a sign that corresponds to a different part of each season.

* **Cardinal:** Aries, as the first fire sign, is the harbinger of spring, and the spring equinox begins the astrological year. Aries is called a cardinal fire sign because it leads the season.

* **Fixed:** Leo, the second fire sign, occurs in midsummer when summer is well established. Leo is a fixed fire sign. The fixed signs are definite, motivated by principles, and powerfully stubborn.
* **Mutable:** Sagittarius is the sign that brings us from one season to the next. Sagittarius moves us from autumn to winter. These signs are called mutable. In terms of character the mutable signs are changeable and flexible.

If you know your element and whether you are a cardinal, fixed, or mutable sign, you know a lot about yourself. This is invaluable for self-care and is reflected in the customized fire sign self-care rituals found in Part 2.

Fire Signs and Self-Care

Self-care is incredibly important for fire signs. But learning how to set aside time for self-care takes discipline because fire doesn't want to stop. Fire elements have an incredible spark that lights up their minds, bodies, and spirits, but, as with fire, those born under this element frequently burn out. When this happens, making frequent pit stops to refuel, rest, and engage in self-care activities that are personalized for their element—like the ones found in Part 2—are what fire signs require to be stoked back to life.

Fire signs need to keep in mind that their self-care activities should be fun and varied; they don't want to get bored doing the same thing over and over again when there are so many different self-care options to try! The fire element crackles with enthusiasm and good spirits, and the more activity, socializing, and fun they can have, the better they like it and the easier it is for people born under this element to get fired up. Fire signs will easily follow any practice or activity that enhances playfulness. Variety in exercise, diet, décor, fashion, friendship, vacations, and socializing gives all fire elements the motivation to enjoy life, and without a good time, life is a misery for these bold personalities.

The best way to approach self-care for fire signs is to make it a game. The fire signs have willpower to follow through on a plan if they decide something is worthwhile and they can enjoy it. The rules of the "game" don't matter as much as the sense of achieving a good score, beating the competition, or enjoying the process. For example, if a fire sign decides to do 10,000 steps in a day and finds at 5 p.m. that he is 1,000 steps short, his motivation to reach his goal would help him find a fun way to complete the program. Perhaps he will decide to march to music, skip, or hop his way to 10,000. A fire sign will get what he needs in two different ways through this type of self-care: he both wins the game and has fun doing it!

Maintaining that flame and steady inspiration is the goal of any self-care program. Play the game of taking care of your body, mind, and spirit, and not only will you benefit from your efforts, but you will also inspire others to follow you.

So now that you know what fire signs need to practice self-care, let's look at each of the fiery characteristics of Sagittarius and how he can maintain his flame.

CHAPTER 4

SELF-CARE FOR SAGITTARIUS

✳

Dates: November 22–December 21
Element: Fire
Polarity: Yang
Quality: Mutable
Symbol: Centaur
Ruler: Jupiter

Sagittarius is the third (and final) fire sign of the zodiac. His time period ushers us from autumn to the winter solstice around December 21. He is yang and mutable, and his preferred self-care rituals line up with the traits associated with these cosmic designations. Sagittarius is the open, adventure-some, optimistic, good-humored sign of the zodiac, and his breezy ease attracts people and luck.

Sagittarius's symbol is the Centaur: half horse (beast) and half man. The centaurs figured in Greek mythology as a band of beasts given to riotous living and fighting, representing the unruly forces of nature. However, the leader of the centaurs was Chiron, a wise and skilled teacher and healer. He tutored the hero Achilles as well as the healer Asclepius. Like these two different versions of the centaur, Sagittarius metaphorically straddles two poles: one representing instinctive natural animal instincts and one the higher mind that quests for meaning and understanding. This sign's symbol outlines the soul journey of Sagittarius: from an instinctual and perhaps unruly character to a perceptive truth-seeking healer, teacher, and philosopher, like Chiron. Additionally, the arrows that the Centaur shoots were not part of the original Greek myth, but in astrology the Centaur shoots "his arrow into the air though he knows not his destiny." The Archer shoots arrows of truth.

Self-Care and Sagittarius

Sagittarius is ruled (and protected) by Jupiter, the planet and, in Roman mythology, chief god. The optimism of Jupiter (the planet is known as the Greater Benefic in astrology) is boundless. Jupiter also represents bigness and excess, and Sagittarius loves having and doing more than enough—which means that taking some time out for self-care is necessary for the Centaur. Roaming the big wide world is Sagittarius's joy. He may not know why he wants to keep moving, but like a nomad he keeps going forward. Sagittarius is wonderful to be around because he rarely says, "We can't do that." His response is usually, "Let's go." The types of self-care that really speak to Sagittarius are typically ones that are full of physicality and movement.

And, at some point, as with Chiron, those born under this fire sign will seek out wisdom and become interested in the workings of the higher mind. The wanderlust, the urge for new horizons, turns inward. Sagittarius is not interested in any one particular religion or practice and is not dogmatic about his beliefs. His great interest is how to live life in accord with the wisdom of the ages and the superconscious mind, rather than the everyday conscious mind. Intuitions become very strong, and, frequently, Sagittarians become counselors, teachers, philanthropists, or humanitarian workers. Sagittarius wants to practice self-care because more restoration and well-being means more energy for life.

Sagittarius is generally rather unconcerned about his appearance, and vanity will not motivate him to practice the ritual of self-care. Looking good for him is the result of an interesting life and not a goal in and of itself. His style is casual. Any self-care item or practice has to be easy and portable. If Sag can put it in a suitcase, he will probably bring it along. If there is too much effort involved, whatever the helpful device is will be left on the hall table.

Sagittarius Rules the Hips and Thighs

Sagittarius rules over the hips and thighs, so self-care related to these parts of the body is especially important. For Sagittarius these muscles and bones are essential for free and easy motion. You may notice that even in a petite

Sagittarian the thighs are very well developed. This is the first area to address in terms of self-care. Stretching is essential and usually something that Sagittarius forgets to do. If he can remember to stretch and then exercise, it will save trouble down the road.

Sagittarius is prone to sciatic stress because the sciatic nerve runs from the base of the spine through the buttocks and down the lower limbs. The best exercise for a Sagittarian, at any age, is walking. He needs to imagine he is going on a journey even if it is just around the block.

Sagittarius and Self-Care Success

Pitfalls for Sag self-care fall mainly around his habit of procrastination. He gets involved in the next adventure or trip, while putting off focusing long enough beforehand on his self-care requirements to see that taking good care of his body, and mind, will only enhance the pleasure of traveling. He is too likely to say, "Oh, I didn't know that flight was 15 hours" as he unkinks his back. He accepts these things with good humor, but taking the time to actively tune into his body's needs will save a lot of stress and wear and tear.

Sag is also in the habit of talking about something (including self-care) before doing it. There seems to be a direct ratio between how much Sagittarius speaks about something and how little he does about it. If he directs his forces to think, meditate, and imagine the desired goal, then there is a good chance he will follow through. If he dissipates his energy in describing, telling everyone what he is going to do, or verbally wondering if he should do it, probably not much will happen.

The best advice for Sag is this: do it; don't talk about it.

Sagittarius is usually not interested in delving into his emotional past and finding reasons for current behavior. But he does like to talk out his thoughts and, in this way, a therapist and good listener can be helpful. Many communication or getting-along-with-people problems for Sagittarius are because he has a peculiar habit of "foot-in-mouth" syndrome: whatever comes to mind comes out of his mouth. His blunt way of speaking rubs most people the wrong way, though he never intends to be mean or hurtful. He just calls it like he sees it and is incapable of lying. This is a characteristic of a Sagittarian, but everyone usually forgives him because he is so genuinely surprised that he has given offense. Awareness of this tendency may push away some of the worst blunders. Jupiter, Sagittarius's ruling planet, is the culprit here. Jupiter rules all excess, whether it is speaking too much, or eating and drinking too much. Sagittarius expresses himself widely and fully, and the more energy he has to give to everything the better. When this energy is used for more hospitality and generosity, he and everyone is pleased. If it leans toward the more destructive feelings, this energy makes chaos and the Centaur can be out of control.

A primary factor in self-care is for Sagittarius to avoid sitting at a desk all day long. This will give back problems, make the Centaur unruly and fidgety, and put him and everyone near him in a bad mood. A standing desk, or a cubicle where he can move around, is the solution. Sagittarius is one of the most common signs of professional athletes. Sagittarius's quick-fire power gives him a fast reaction time as well as stamina. Self-care is easy for a Sagittarian professional athlete because his performance is tied to his profession. And his strength is that he never hews to a rigid schedule or regime. His instincts tell him what needs stretching and strengthening. This is a good reminder for non-athlete Sagittarians too.

Perhaps the most important pathway for self-care success for Sagittarius, however, is laughter! If a Centaur can see and feel the humor in whatever self-care activity he is involved in, then the practice will be successful. Sharing jokes and laughter with buddies will encourage Sagittarius and everyone around him. His laughter is contagious and self-care is the best way to increase it. So let's take a look at some restorative self-care activities designed especially for you, Sagittarius.

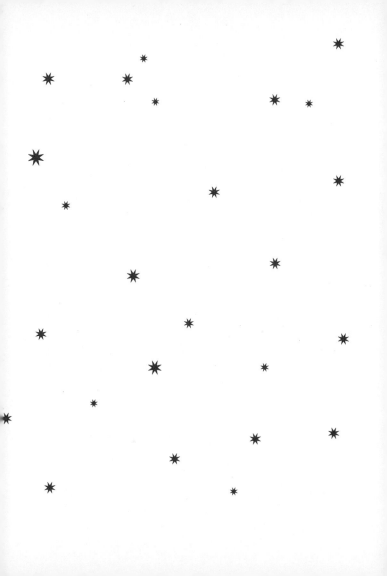

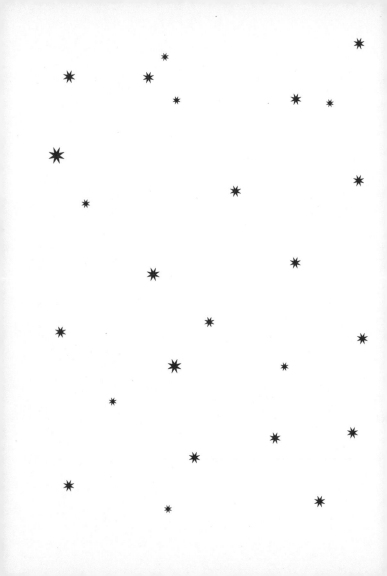

PART 2

SELF-CARE
RITUALS
— FOR —
SAGITTARIUS

Sweat Your Way to Relaxation

———————

While we often think of heat as linked to passion and intensity, it can also be incredibly restorative and relaxing for fire signs. Embrace the calming effect of heat by seeking out a sauna at your local gym or spa. Take time to lounge in the warmth, allowing the sweat to cleanse your body of impurities. Breathe in the heat and feel it soften your muscles and increase your circulation. As the warmth envelopes your body, any pain and stress will melt away.

Can't find a sauna nearby? No problem. Turn on your shower to hot and let the water run for a few minutes. Be sure to close your windows and bathroom doors. Then get a comfy seat and kick back in your own at-home sauna for some rest and recuperation.

Try Deep-Tissue Massage
for Ultimate Relief

Do your sore muscles need a little TLC? Soothing touch is a great way to alleviate stress in your body and your mind. As a fire sign, ignite a different type of heat inside you by turning to the therapeutic benefits of deep-tissue massage. The warmth created by kneading muscle tissue and improved blood circulation can ease chronic tension, pain, and stiffness. And this deeply therapeutic ritual can help calm anxiety and worry as well.

Place your trust in an experienced massage therapist. Before your massage starts, tell them exactly how your body feels and what it needs to get better. Keep in mind that a deep-tissue massage should never be painful, so don't be afraid to speak up at any point during your massage. Communication is key.

Promote Strong Bones and Muscles with Figs

———————————

Delicious and full of potassium, figs are the perfect ingredient for the healthy, energized Sagittarius. Sagittarius controls the hips and thighs, and a strong body is essential to the adventurous Centaur. If he doesn't move around enough during the day, the pressure on his hips can lead to muscle pain and cramps.

You can help to prevent these aches and discomfort with the potassium found in figs. Figs are a Sagittarius fruit, and the potassium strengthens muscles and preserves the calcium in your bones. Cut fresh figs into a salad with leafy greens and other restorative ingredients such as almonds and pure honey.

Begin (and End) Projects with a Bang

Sagittarius is motivated by the energy and excitement of his surroundings. While others might get by with a quick crossing out of a completed task, Sagittarius needs something with a bit more panache to celebrate the small victories—or get in the zone for a new project. Decorate your work area with a small gong and strike it before and after completing a task. The simple but energizing melody will be just the motivation you need to get things done.

Strike a Pilates Pose

Pilates is the perfect exercise for the athletic Sagittarius. It stretches and builds lean muscles, and provides a ritual of discipline that keeps him grounded. As the sign that controls the thighs and hips, Sagittarius will delight in exercises that target these parts of the body. A great exercise for your thighs and hips is the leg bridge combined with leg dips. Form a bridge with your legs by lying on your back with your feet flat on the floor (arms at your sides) and lifting your hips off the floor. Extend one leg up and out so it is perpendicular to your torso, and then lower and repeat with the other leg.

Burn Up the Competition

Fire signs thrive off of a little friendly competition—the key word being friendly! Engage your fiery competitive side in a healthy way by joining a community sports league of your choosing. You may find that team sports, like soccer, kickball, basketball, volleyball, or even a running group, suit you best. The sense of comradery can jump-start that passion inside you for action. Use the energy and excitement coming from your teammates as fuel. Just remember, it's only a game. No matter if your team wins or loses, the primary goal is to have fun and get your body moving.

Teach That Learning Is Power

It's as simple as ABC... As a fire sign, your ambition and passion for adventure has given you a lot of life experiences. Bring that passion and spirit you have for life to others by volunteering as a teacher in one capacity or another. This may mean becoming a mentor at a local after-school program, reading to children at the library, or teaching adults a special skill like painting or accounting at a community center. The choice is yours. But however you choose to go about it, know that instilling knowledge in others is an act of love and patience. A good teacher can inspire and motivate their students. And the benefit isn't just theirs. As a fire sign, engaging with a group can be incredibly fulfilling for you too. Take a survey of your many talents and see where you can help.

Learn a New Language

Curious and energetic, Sagittarius loves to learn and travel. Learning a new language will challenge your mind, while arousing your wanderlust. Many smartphone apps offer language lessons for users of all skill levels. There are also countless books and classes out there if you prefer a more traditional approach to learning.

Before jetting off on your next adventure, take some time to learn at least the basics of the native language in that region. Not only will you enjoy learning something new, but an understanding of basic words and phrases will open you up to meeting and communicating with people of different cultural backgrounds during your travels.

Engage in a Little Philanthropy

Jupiter, Sagittarius's ruler, governs generosity and involvement in worthy causes. Sagittarius loves helping those in need, and also appreciates the different perspectives he gains through his philanthropy. Make a conscious choice to contribute to any organization or charity that you feel reflects your values and ideals. No matter how much you have to share, spread your generosity with the world! Your help will be greatly appreciated, and you may learn a few new things in the process.

Soak Up the Sun

It's time to turn up the heat! Fire signs need vacations just like everyone else, but when planning yours, stick to warm, sunny destinations. You need the heat to feed your soul. Ditch your coat and look for vacation spots on the beach or in the desert, where the sun is strong and the temperatures soar. Fire signs are nourished by the heat, so soak up the rays for ultimate replenishment.

Keep your body and mind challenged with tons of adventures and new experiences. While taking some time to lounge and relax is totally fine, you need something to get your fire burning. Try to schedule at least one activity each day you are on vacation, whether that means going for a hike through canyons or learning to surf. The more out of your comfort zone you are, the more alive you'll feel.

Communicate with Your Fellow Equine

The Centaur, the symbol of Sagittarius, is half horse and half human. Realign with your celestial heritage—and also feel the wind through your mane—by taking a horseback ride (or consider a lesson)! An adventurous gallop on the back of a horse will delight your playful side and celebrate your love of the natural world. Too hot or cold outside for a ride? Visit a horse ranch or farm rescue and devote an afternoon to grooming or mucking out the stalls for your hooved companions.

Make 'Em Laugh

There's nothing quite like the power of a good belly laugh. Fire signs are extroverts by nature and love to entertain people with stories, songs, and even jokes. While you may not have an entire stand-up comedy set ready to go yet, all it takes is one simple joke to get someone laughing and improve their day. And that rush of joy coursing through your veins as your audience laughs is enough to raise any fire sign's temperature. Don't know any good jokes off the top of your head? Go for the classics or search online for some new material. And remember, it's all in the delivery!

Calm Your Mind with Jasmine

Keep a jasmine plant in your home, preferably in your bedroom or any other room where you like to relax. It's the perfect plant for Sagittarius as it promotes calm and restful sleep, which will leave him well rested and ready for the exciting day ahead.

A simple flower, jasmine brings a touch of nature's beauty into the Sagittarian home. Caring for your plant is simple: just water weekly and add a wire frame or wooden pole to the pot for support once the vines have started to grow out.

Journal Your Daily Reflections

Sagittarius has so much on his mind, from past adventures, to future plans and reflections on life. Keep a journal to chronicle all of these thoughts and memories. You can start a nightly ritual of jotting down everything that you experienced or felt that day, or devote some time at the end of each week to reflect on everything that has happened since your last entry. You can write about your adventures with friends, your feelings and opinions, your personal philosophies, or whatever else comes to mind.

Focus on the Flame

Fire signs are drawn to the sacred element inside them: the flame. From the blue center to the red-hot aura glowing outward, the flame calls you on an instinctual level. Use the power of fire to keep yourself balanced when you need it most. At times of high stress, find a quiet respite. Light a candle of your choosing and sit in front of it. Watch as the flame dances, softly flickering as it burns slowly. Take solace in the beauty of the flame before you, allowing the whole world to fall away around you. It is just you and the flame. Fix your gaze on the flame as it flares and sways, and try to quiet your mind as best as possible. If you find your mind wandering, don't worry. Gently return your focus to the flame in front of you. Repeat for as long as you wish or until the flame has extinguished.

Find Your Passion

———————

Discovering what kindles the passion inside you usually comes naturally for fire signs. After all you are full of strong emotions and big ideas, all of which drive your sense of knowing and well-being. Maybe it's a hobby that makes your heart sing, or a political cause, or a person. Hone in on those things and make them a prominent part of your life if they aren't already. Indulge in the passion you feel for them, and let it fill you with meaning and support. If you are unsure about what lights your fire, it's time to start learning about yourself. Try a new meal, make a new friend, read a new book. Your journey of self-discovery will lead you to your true passions.

Relax in Velvet

Jupiter, Sagittarius's ruling planet, is linked to the love of things a bit indulgent and luxurious, including silky, plush fabrics. Restore your Jupiter roots with the most luxe of all textiles: velvet! Spend an afternoon wrapped in a velvet robe, enjoying the smooth, soft fabric on your skin, to feel like the planetary royalty you are. You can also go a bit further by purchasing velvet bedding, but beware: it won't be easy to get out of this heavenly bed in the morning.

Visit a Place of Worship

Sagittarius represents the quest for spiritual enlightenment and the celebration of different religious traditions. Refocus your quest by experiencing a devotional ceremony at your chosen place of worship. Meditate in a Buddhist temple, pray in a mosque, sing a hymn in a church pew, or chant in front of a Hindu shrine.

No matter which devotional practice you observe, your experience will activate your crown chakra (the connection between your own consciousness and the energy of the universe around you) and further you on your journey to spiritual understanding.

Visit a Sacred Historic Site

Combine your Sagittarian wanderlust and quest for spiritual enlightenment with a pilgrimage to a sacred location. Researching thoroughly first, you could visit the Temple Mount in Jerusalem, Israel; one (or all four) of the Char Dham pilgrimage sites in India; the Great Mosque of Muhammad Ali Pasha in Cairo, Egypt; Saint Peter's Basilica in Rome, Italy; the Bodh Gaya in Bihar, India; or the city of Bethlehem in Palestine—or plan an extended trip to visit them all! These are just a few of the myriad of famous spiritual locations across the world that you can explore.

Plan an International Getaway

Always keep your passport up to date and ready to use. Sagittarius is the king of adventure, so a trip abroad is the perfect balm for a chaotic or dull workweek. If a release from the hustle and bustle of the office is what you seek, opt for a soothing beachside retreat with a tropical beverage and plenty of sunscreen. Looking for some excitement after an uneventful week? A revitalizing trip to the colorful avenues of Barcelona, or a zip-lining excursion through a rainforest, will be just what the doctor ordered.

Flirt

Intimacy and sexual connection are key components in a relationship, especially for fire signs. You live to feel close to others and make your passion for them known in one way or another. When the mood strikes, unleash your inner flirt and have some fun with the person you are smitten with. Bat your eyes. Whisper sweet nothings. Tell them a corny joke. Let loose and show your unique personality.

Combine Earth and Fire

S tone is one of the earth's most sacred elements, and with a touch of heat, it becomes the ultimate healing tool. You can benefit from the combination of these two elements by indulging in a hot-stone massage.

Fire signs are naturally active beings, often pushing their bodies to the limit with exercise and adventure. Take time to let your body relax and heal after strenuous activity, and why not do so with a soothing hot-stone massage? Not only do the stones connect with the primal fire inside you, but they expand your blood vessels, improving circulation and flushing your skin, all while relaxing sore muscles.

Try Spontaneity

When is the last time you did something completely on impulse? Hopefully not too long ago, because enthusiastic spontaneity is the ruling philosophy for all fire signs. Have you been feeling a little trapped lately? Stuck in a rut you just can't break free from? Don't ignore that little voice inside you urging you to do something a little out of your comfort zone. Being impulsive and spontaneous electrifies the fire sign's soul and feeds the energy within. Without it, you'll suffocate under the weight of predictability.

Visit the Racetrack

It's a thrill to watch, connects you with your equine symbol, and employs your Sagittarian luck. For an added layer of excitement, attend one of the big races: the Kentucky Derby, Preakness Stakes, or Belmont Stakes. Taking place in the spring each year in Kentucky, Maryland, and New York respectively, these races have deep roots in American tradition. Racegoers often dress up in eye-catching pastels and oversized hats, and enjoy signature cocktails like the Mint Julep, Black-Eyed Susan, and Belmont Breeze.

Revisit a Favorite Comedy

When you're in need of emotional release, turn to your favorite laugh-out-loud comedy. It may seem counterintuitive, but a funny movie is actually one of the best ways a fire sign can let go of any nasty emotions that have been building up over time. You have so much passion swirling inside you that you need a positive way to let it all out. If you have a favorite comedy, turn it on—or if you want to try something new, check out what's playing at your local theater. Need more of a reason to laugh? Not only does laughter help reduce stress hormones in your body, it also helps increase immune cells and releases endorphins, the body's feel-good chemical. Win-win!

Set a Fitness Goal

Sagittarius has a sustained fire power that few can hold a flame to. When a busy work schedule pushes physical self-care to the wayside, that fire longs to get out, and you may feel tension in your muscles from the lack of exercise. Having a long-term fitness goal will push you to dedicate that much-needed time each week to taking care of your body, so you can achieve whatever dream you set your sights on. Consider training for a marathon, a trek up Mount Kilimanjaro, or a CrossFit competition.

Make a List

_____

Fire signs often have a lot of great ideas and like to start a variety of projects when inspiration strikes. It's just part of the territory—you are naturally creative and dream big. The hurdle is completing these projects.

Take a survey of your life and make note of different projects or plans that are sitting around half-finished. Make a list of everything you want to complete and when you want to complete them by. You can be as specific or as vague as you want.

Maybe that wine rack you are building doesn't need to be finished for another year or so, or maybe you want to show off your favorite bottles by next month. The ultimate goal is committing to expectations and following through on your plans. And just imagine how much better you'll feel once you've checked off a few of those projects from your list.

Burn, Baby, Burn

Fire is cathartic for fire signs. It can cleanse and purify your energy, and helps you let go of emotional burdens. From destruction comes regrowth, better and stronger than before.

Use the natural destruction inherent with fire to your advantage. Write down your feelings on a few pieces of paper. Light a candle and place it in a fire-safe bowl or in the sink. Carefully hold each piece of paper to the flame and allow it to catch fire. Watch as fire consumes your words and emotions. Drop the piece of paper into the sink or bowl to continue burning. As each emotion goes up in flames, feel the weight on your heart lessen. You are free, ready to rise from the ashes more resilient and determined.

Sleep It Off

A good night's sleep can be transformative, but, unfortunately, fire signs often have a hard time getting enough sleep for their own good. As a fire sign, you naturally need less sleep than others, but that doesn't mean you are invincible. It just means you have to work a little harder at giving yourself the best chance possible for restorative sleep. With all the activity you do every day, you need your rest.

Creating a good sleep routine is key. Take note of how you usually get ready for bed. Do you already have a routine, or does it change from night to night? Do you have a specific bedtime you shoot for, or do you stay up until different times depending on your mood?

To help stabilize your sleep schedule, try implementing a few easy, enjoyable activities you can do right before bed, anything from reading for a few minutes before closing your eyes to taking a long bath, or even meditating. Aim to get into bed at around the same time every night.

Shake Those Hips
(and Thighs)

Sagittarius rules the hips and thighs. Give these parts of your body a proper workout to keep them strong and ready for adventure. Ideal workouts that allow you to really shake those hips (and thighs) in a fun way are those that incorporate dancing, such as Zumba and Buti Yoga. These faster-paced routines get your blood pumping and your muscles working in an exciting way that you'll forget is exercise. You can also bring friends along for even more fun! If working out in a group setting isn't your style, there are many online videos and entire video games out there for dance-focused fitness that you can do in your own home.

Read a Classic

———————

A classic novel is a perfect way to stimulate the Sagittarian love for philosophical and reflective thought. Great places to start include the works of Jane Austen, Mark Twain, and Charles Dickens. During or after your read, you can spark further thought with online guided questions (some books also include discussion group questions right in the back of the book). Consider having a friend or two read the same title as well so you can discuss your thoughts and insights with one another after reading.

Avoid Burnout

With all the complicated emotions you hold onto as a fire sign, it can sometimes be helpful to seek out a professional therapist to work through your thoughts. Talking to a professional is often a therapeutic experience and can promote overall wellness in your life. Fire signs are prone to emotional fatigue and burnout because their emotions run intensely for extended periods of time. It can drain your system to keep them bottled up. Eventually, you'll run out of gas. Turning to a trained professional who can help you understand and sort your stressors can save your emotional well-being and give you a healthy outlet to better yourself.

Take a Staycation

Sagittarius has a natural sense of wanderlust, but sometimes the excitement is happening right outside your door! Don't miss out on what your town or region has to offer. A "staycation" is the perfect way to explore in a local, less stressful, way. Check out any websites for your area that list upcoming events—or host an event of your own for neighbors. You can also invite friends who don't live locally to visit and share the wonderful aspects of your area with them!

Find a Sagittarius Totem

A totem is a small object that represents anything from a person or group of people, to a personal value or ideology. Whether it's tied to the equine symbol (a Centaur or horse) of your astrological sign, or to the archery element (a bow or arrow), find a totem that encapsulates your zodiac sign. Your totem will be a unique symbol of your amazing Sagittarian qualities, from your humor and warmth to your intelligence and courage. Look to it when you need a little reminder of just how exceptional you are.

Change It Up

Predictability is the fire sign's ultimate enemy. How do you avoid getting stuck in the same humdrum pattern? Change things up. Start in your home, where you spend the majority of your time and where you feel the most comfortable.

To get the winds of change blowing, open your windows (if you can) and move your furniture around into different arrangements in all of your major spaces. This could mean moving your bed from one wall to the other or changing which direction your couch faces. It could also mean doing something as small as adding a piece of furniture to a room. Whatever feels right to you! Sometimes just changing your perspective can make all the difference in the world.

Streamline Your Space

Clutter can do more than just cause a mess in your home. It can overwhelm your mind and make you feel trapped. Fire signs love big spaces with a lot of room to move around. If you find that you are feeling claustrophobic in your own living space, it might be time to streamline your belongings.

Start by going through your closets and cabinets and throw out anything you don't need. Next, move on to your furniture. Many fire signs find the minimalist design aesthetic a pleasing choice. Look for furniture that does double duty, like a combination desk and dining table. The most important thing is to give yourself space to feel free.

Take the Horse Stance

This yoga pose is perfect for Sagittarius—and not just because of the name! This Horse Stance improves posture and strengthens the thigh muscles, which are ruled by the athletic Centaur. From a standing position, move your feet apart slightly wider than shoulder-distance apart, toes pointing outward. As you inhale, reach your arms overhead wide, pressing your palms together. As you exhale, bend your knees 90 degrees and pull your hands to your chest, sliding your shoulder blades downward. Keep your knees pointed over your feet and your tailbone tucked under your body. Hold this pose for 30 seconds, or however long you can manage, and remember to breathe.

Follow Your Intuition

———————

Your intuition is invaluable when it comes to decision-making. Fire signs often move from one idea to the next rather quickly, but your gut reaction to an idea can help inform whether you should pursue it or not. You don't have the time to sit and weigh the pros and cons, using your mind to decide. You use your heart and that feeling pulsing inside either urging you forward or calling out warnings to stop. Listen to that voice. It tells the most primal truths about your journey as a person, and its only purpose is to help you navigate through life's confusing moments.

Still aren't sure what your intuition is telling you? Sometimes, it can even be a physical feeling. Do you get a warm rush in your veins when you think of something? Or is it more of a stomachache? Our bodies have different ways of speaking to us. Listen for yours.

Take an Archery Lesson

Translated from Latin as "the arrow," Sagittarius's signature sport is written in the stars! Learn the basic techniques of archery one afternoon—or turn it into a regular hobby! Requiring precision and practice, this sport is the perfect way to release your Sagittarian energy—and a few arrows too. Archery also enhances physical strength and concentration (hitting your target is not as easy as the Centaur makes it seem), so on-the-go Sagittarius will be ready for anything.

Daydream

Both philosophical and curious, Sagittarius understands the need for reflection between adventures. Take a moment to pause and let your mind wander. The deepest thoughts and realizations can often come from directionless meditation. To begin, you can concentrate on an object nearby, letting your thoughts take over in any way they please. You can also start by asking yourself a question: What are my current life goals? Who do I look to for advice and why? Where would I go right now if I could travel anywhere on (or beyond) earth? Be as specific or vague as you want, and invite in any thought that arises.

Ride a Bike

Unable to take a horseback ride? Go for a spin on your bicycle. Look for a hill that is safe for riding so you can really fly. Whether racing a friend or yourself—down a mountain trail or a driveway—the feeling of speed and of fresh air swirling past your face is made for Sagittarius. Just be sure to put on a helmet before you start training for the next Tour de France!

Don't Test Your Limits

F ire signs have a tendency to overexert themselves, physically and emotionally. Because of this it's important to recognize your limits, and to try not to push them too much. If you find you have a propensity for going too far emotionally, it might be time to create a list of warning signs that you can flag for yourself. When you see those warning signs popping up in your thought pattern and behavior, or if you feel yourself getting too stressed and overwhelmed, schedule a self-care activity to help find equilibrium once again. It can be as simple as taking a bath or visiting an old friend.

If you push yourself athletically, always give your body time to recuperate. While fire signs always want to go farther and be better physically, not allowing your body to rest after physical exertion can increase your risk for serious injury. Don't let your fire burn too bright—you are your own best advocate for balance and well-being.

Keep a Dream Journal

Sagittarius rules the higher mind, which gains insights into your deeper consciousness and purpose through dreams and other internal experiences. Use a dream journal to keep track of your dreams so you can better understand your needs, desires, and fears, and how they influence your daily life.

Note the main elements of your dream: Was there a recurring item or emotion? How does this dream relate to past dreams? Is this the first time that a certain animal has appeared in your dreams, or has it emerged before? Dozens of websites and books out there can then help you decipher what specific dream elements mean.

Embrace H$_2$O

Water and fire are opposites. And while water can extinguish fire, those born as fire signs need water to keep them thriving and succeeding. With all the strenuous activities you do as a fire sign, don't forget to keep hydrated. It can be easy to forget to stop and drink water when you are focused on achieving a physical goal. Make it a priority to drink the recommended number of ounces of water a day, and more if you are engaging in demanding physical workouts. Remember that water will not smother the flame burning inside of you.

Beat the Heat

Balance can be the key to a happy life. As a fire sign, you must learn to offset your heat and passion with coolness. Begin with how you nourish your body. If it feels like your inner fire is burning too hot, put away the spices and try to balance the heat by eating cooling foods. Turn to foods such as watermelon, cucumber, and yogurt, and if you are feeling really indulgent, ice cream. The cool contrast will help keep your inner fire from burning out of control.

Enjoy a Night on the Town

Your Sagittarian humor and buoyant spirit attract many different kinds of people to you, but sometimes even the magnetic, warm Sagittarius can feel a little less than his awesome self. Invite a group of friends out for a night of lighthearted fun—and maybe a dare or two—to remember just how loved you are. Whether it involves a trip to the latest "it" club or ordering one of every appetizer at a favorite restaurant, it will be a night that neither you nor your friends forget.

Take a Class

———————

Sagittarius is the sign of curiosity and learning. Exercise your mental muscles with a continuing education class at a local college, or an online course that piques your interest. Topics that Sagittarius will enjoy exploring include philosophy, spirituality, elements of the natural world, and different cultures. Try a class on the teachings of Plato, the notion of reincarnation, identifying different plant species in a certain region, or the rites of passage in the Apache culture.

Try the Ancient Power of Hot Yoga

B ikram yoga is a form of yoga done in an environment where the temperature is about 104°F. Heat is a vital element of this exercise. Practicing yoga in a heated room is a great way to potentially increase your metabolism and your heart rate, which in turn allows your blood vessels to expand and your muscles to become more flexible.

This form of hot yoga is perfect for fire signs. Fire signs feed off of the heat around them, and use it to find equilibrium and balance. Look for hot yoga classes near you to challenge yourself and your body. If you've never tried a hot yoga class before, be sure to hydrate your body beforehand and to bring a small towel with you to class. Get ready to sweat!

Draw a Bath

As a fire sign, you already have a special affinity to heat and its galvanizing power. But it is also a wonderful relaxation tool. Warm water can be incredibly soothing for a weary fire sign. If your mind is cluttered from the demands of day-to-day life, and your muscles are sore from all of the physical activities you do, climb into a warm bath and let the water alleviate your ailments.

You can even add a special bath bomb or bubbles to the bath to make it more relaxing. Go for scents like lavender, jasmine, or even rose to ease your mind. Adding Epsom salt to the warm water can help take the ache out of overused muscles. Start by adding 1 cup of Epsom salt to the bath as the water runs.

Enlist in Boot Camp

Boot camp–style exercise classes are popular fitness options for fire signs looking to add a little heat to their typical workout regime. These boot camps attract a wide variety of people, and the group atmosphere can really ignite a spark for fire signs who love a little friendly competition. You'll learn to encourage others to push their physical limit, and to push your own limit as well. The combination of intense cardiovascular or strength-training exercises with a supportive team dynamic can be a rewarding experience for many fire signs. Make friends, build muscle, and tone your heart, all at the same time.

Enjoy Fireside Chats

The fireplace is often the center of the home. It's where people gather together to keep warm and to share stories. As a fire sign, you have an innate connection to fireplaces—they feel comfortable to you, like old friends. If you have a fireplace in your home, make it the center of your space. Arrange seating around the fireplace so it becomes the focal point. Use it as often as you can to take advantage of your sacred connection to the fire it contains.

If you don't have a fireplace already, you can often buy a decorative, portable fireplace from many home goods stores. Just the look of fire dancing can pacify a stressed-out fire sign. If you can't have any sort of fireplace, decorative or not, in your home, look for a restaurant or bar nearby that has one and make that your new go-to spot for drinks, dinner, and cozy relaxation.

Relax under an Oak Tree

Sacred to the Sagittarian ruler Jupiter, oak has represented the link between the spiritual and natural worlds since ancient Greece and Rome. Reacquaint yourself with the great outdoors—and your planetary ruler—by stretching out under an oak tree or climbing its branches (you do love adventure).

Those past civilizations also saw oak as a protective charm, and the mythological Greek warrior Jason of the Argonauts used a sacred oak branch in the building of his ship *Argo* before sailing off to battle. Part archer himself, Sagittarius has a unique connection to nature that can easily be forgotten in the chaos of everyday life. A simple afternoon enjoying the shade and splendor of an oak will leave you feeling refreshed and realigned with your Sagittarian spirit.

Go on a Digital Detox

Fire signs are always moving from one thing to the next. That's because they are ambitious and motivated, traits that can sometimes lead to some serious burnout if you aren't careful.

One way to purposefully give yourself a break from the fast pace of the world around you is to unplug digitally as often as possible. Try and put your phone or tablet away at the same time every night, approximately an hour before bedtime. This gives your mind time to unwind before sleep.

If you go on vacation, consider switching your phone on just once a day to check for urgent messages. At home, designate a basket for devices and ask that family members place their phones and tablets in it before time meant to be spent together. And when going to dinner with friends, focus on enjoying your food and company—not keeping one eye on your phone at all times.

Create a Vision Board

Sagittarius is a dreamer. Create a visual board to capture all of your big plans and desires onto something tangible that you can keep in a place such as your bedroom or office to look at on a daily basis. When you are constantly reminded of the things you aspire to, you will feel motivated to continue taking steps to reach those goals, even when they may feel further away. No matter how big or small, those steps add up, and before you know it, you will be manifesting the dreams on your vision board into reality.

Get a Good Night's Sleep

As the vivacious explorer, Sagittarius is always on the move. Make sure you get a good night's sleep before and after your adventures. No Centaur can perform his best when he is constantly yawning and needing caffeine pick-me-ups! Consider investing in a humidifier or dehumidifier if too much or too little moisture in the air makes it difficult for you to fall or stay asleep. You can also diffuse lavender oil or spray it (diluted according to instructions) onto your pillow to help you relax and get into the bedtime mind-set.

Catch Some Rays

S pending time outside soaking up the sun can lift any fire sign's mood. Think of yourself as a solar panel. You need the sunlight to reenergize your soul when you are feeling depleted. Lucky for fire signs, sunlight can help increase serotonin levels—those feel-good chemicals in your brain—thus boosting your happy mood.

Take some time to bathe in the sun, letting the rays wash over you. Feel the warmth on your skin, and imagine the sunshine penetrating down into your heart, lighting you up on the inside. Bask in the warmth around you.

While sun exposure, at the right times and intensity, can be beneficial for anyone, too much sun can be dangerous, even if you are a fire sign. Always take the proper precautions while out recharging in the sun, like wearing sunscreen and remembering to reapply.

Burn Myrrh

An ancient spice connected to Sagittarius, myrrh has been a part of spiritual practices and worship since ancient Egypt. The sign of spiritual enlightenment, Sagittarius will feel opened to the intangible elements of the universe when burning this herb. Jupiter, Sagittarius's ruler, governs the liver, which myrrh has been used to detoxify since the beginning of traditional Chinese medicine. You can burn myrrh gum powder and myrrh resin incense with an incense bowl or censer and a charcoal tablet. Myrrh can also be found as an essential oil to diffuse or, diluted according to instructions, to massage into the skin.

Get Creative

Being creative comes naturally to fire signs. They are often temperamental and passionate, and need a healthy way to release the emotions inside of them. While many fire signs turn to physical activities like athletics to help control the blaze within, flexing your creative muscles can be just as beneficial. Try indulging in the creative arts as inspiration. Hobbies such as painting, pottery, coloring, writing, or even knitting or scrapbooking can fuel your creative spark. Get a friend to join you as well. There are tons of ways to let your creativity run free. The only limit is your own imagination.

Take a Trip

———

Fire signs are drawn to impulse and improvisation. If they don't feed their desire for adventure on a regular basis, fire signs can sometimes get cranky and start feeling stuck. To remedy this, cash in your airplane miles and take a last-minute trip to somewhere you've always wanted to visit. Even a last-minute weekend trip to another town nearby can satisfy a fire sign's need for fresh scenery. Your need to explore unfamiliar territory can lead you to great discoveries about yourself and the world around you. Don't let the fear of the unknown stop you. Be spontaneous!

Let's Get Physical

Making time for yourself can be difficult when you are a fire sign. You are always going, going, going, with very little downtime. There's always so much to do, and so little time to do it. Who wants to spend their free time going to the doctor? But, as a fire sign, it's important to make your health a priority. You tend to push yourself both physically and mentally, striving for the next success benchmark. Make sure you keep tabs on your health, and schedule an annual physical checkup with your doctor to make sure you are healthy and strong. Your wellness should never be put on the back burner.

Greet the Day

Whether you are an early bird or a night owl, as a fire sign you have a natural attraction to the sun. You are drawn to its power and heat, and can often generate strength from its rays. Don't ignore this special connection you have with the sun. Embrace its energy and start your day by going for a long morning walk. By beginning the day by communing with the element that speaks to you the most, you can help set the stage for a positive afternoon, evening, and night ahead.

Check In on Your Emotions

Your emotional health is often overlooked when you're a fire sign. You are constantly moving from one thing to the next, so you may not make time to take your emotional temperature. Fire signs also spend a lot of time supporting and entertaining others emotionally. You are the first to step up and help a friend in need, but that concern doesn't transfer to your own well-being. Check in with yourself as often as possible. Are you stressed? Tired? Overwhelmed? Make a list of what you are feeling. If any of those feelings intensify, take some time to practice self-care in whatever form that suits you best.

Just Say No

_____

F ire signs are prone to saying yes to everything, almost to a fault. You tend to move from one activity to the next, accepting the latest invite and helping friends whenever they need. That's wonderful for everyone else, but it also means you burn both ends of your candle, until sometimes the only thing left is ashes. To help keep your fire from going out, practice saying no when you are feeling overextended. This may happen at work, with friends, with your family, or even to yourself. Prioritize your own needs over others. Know there is nothing wrong with taking time to stoke your own flame.

Keep Your Cool

Fire signs can be temperamental at times. It's not your fault. You are naturally feisty and passionate, both positive traits that make you loyal and hard-working. Sometimes, though, you can get a little too overheated. At that point it's important to take a step back before you lose your cool too much. One trick you can try is to count to five in your head, or out loud. An alternate option is to exhale first and then inhale and repeat three times. Either way, you'll give yourself a moment to curtail the strong emotions that are driving you. Practice tamping down the fire within you without letting it go out.

Enjoy the Sunset

———————

The sun is very symbolic for fire signs. Its energy sustains and comforts you, so it's no surprise that watching the sun set after a long day can help you relax and find peace. Find a local spot with a great view if you can, and settle in for a show. Find solace in watching the different colors that emanate across the sky as the sun dips below the horizon: from bright orange, to light pink, soft periwinkle to, finally, a deep blue. Let the phases of its descent remind you that with every ending comes a beginning. The sun goes down, and the sun comes up.

Go for a Ride

Satisfy your fiery sense of adventure with a spontaneous mini-road trip. Take the back roads, avoid the highways, and make this a leisurely trip to clear your mind, ease your spirit, and reignite your wanderlust. You don't necessarily need to have a final destination in mind; just embrace the journey and the open road. As you're driving, you can sing along to your favorite playlist or put on a podcast or audiobook. Take the time alone in your car to enjoy yourself and your surroundings. It does not need to be a lengthy drive in order to experience its benefits—you just need to relax and enjoy the ride.

Go on a Social Media Detox

Fire signs love to live in the moment, but don't ruin that moment by feeling the need to update your social media accounts. By taking a step back from your online presence, you allow yourself to be present and fully experience the world around you. Rather than fearing missing out on the things you see people post about, go out into the world and enjoy them yourself.

Social media can be a great way to stay in touch with friends and family; however, don't let it be the only way you communicate and tend to your relationships. A social media detox allows you to rekindle these connections and share your stories in person.

Go Adventuring
with a Friend

Share your sign with a friend? Take them on an adventure that will invigorate both of your fun-loving personalities. Whether it is a surprise afternoon hike near home or a birthday trip to another region, your friend will cherish the memories always—and you will too. As one of the curious signs of the zodiac, your fondest moments will be in discovering something new together—be it a nest of newly hatched birds along the mountain trail, or a delicious regional cuisine.

Refocus with Amethyst

The amethyst represents the third eye (connected to personal insight) and spirituality, but also temperance and concentration with a clear mind. With so many exciting things to do, Sagittarius can get caught up in a constant shift from one task or thought to the next. A little focus will allow him to keep track of things that need to be done, and to see those projects through to the end. Place an amethyst geode prominently in your work space or living room. Avoid bringing it into a sleeping space, though, as it will be hard to fall asleep when your gears are still turning.

Strike a Work-Life Balance

As a fire sign, you have a passion to succeed in every aspect of your life. While this burning desire to achieve greatness powers your professional performance, it can also cause your work life to take over your whole life. It's important for your overall well-being that you keep your life inside the office balanced with your life outside the office. If you set boundaries between your professional and personal lives, you will be more productive at work and more fulfilled outside of it. You don't want to neglect your work responsibilities, but it's important to disconnect and recharge. By striking this work-life balance, you'll continue to succeed without burning out.

Get Some Fresh Air

Oxygen feeds fire, so when you feel your spark starting to dim, take 10 minutes to go outside and breathe in the fresh air. Whether you're at work or at home, it's the perfect way to take some time for yourself and recharge. As you're enjoying the fresh air, allow yourself to live in that moment. Take a deep, meaningful breath in through your nose, hold for 5 seconds, and breathe out through your mouth. Feel the air fill your lungs and circulate through your body. This simple mindful breathing exercise feeds your internal flame, calms your mind, and reenergizes your spirit.

Clear the Path to Abundance with Turquoise

A good luck charm for health and abundance, turquoise is ruled by auspicious Sagittarius. Carry a small turquoise crystal in your left hand or left pocket for an added boost of luck (yes, you may be quite fortunate already, but a little extra help never hurt).

Throughout history turquoise has also been believed to have metaphysical healing powers. Desiring spiritual understanding and knowledge, Sagittarius may find divine secrets in turquoise. Believed to absorb the energies of the universe, this gem can help you by realigning your own energy centers and balancing them with the energies of the world around you.

Forgive Yourself

As a fire sign, it's easy to go from passionate to incensed. Usually, these feelings are reserved for people who aren't able to keep up with your fiery spirit. However, what happens when you are the one you're upset with? If you've done something that's created your own mental hang-up, you need to extinguish those feelings sooner rather than later. You don't want to be your own worst enemy. While it's important to keep yourself accountable, you also need to be able to forgive yourself for any missteps or mistakes you've made. Release those feelings that have been burning you up inside and channel your energy into positive thoughts and actions.

Write Out Your Thoughts

Fire signs are known for following their gut instincts, but with all the background noise buzzing around you, it can be hard to hone in on what your gut is saying. Try a stream-of-conscious writing exercise to amplify your inner monologue. First, clear your mind. Next, think about something you feel you need guidance on: anything from a career question, to relationships, to personal development. Then just start writing. Don't think too much about what you are writing; just allow the words to flow. Write for as long as you want. In the end you may find the answer you were looking for all along buried within your words.

Spice Things Up

I ntrepid Sagittarius doesn't have time for bland foods—he loves spices and exotic flavors that take his taste buds for a spin. Restore your vibrant energy by adding a delicious cinnamon kick to your warm morning oatmeal, savory dinner casserole—or just about any meal or side dish. Even just a sprinkle in your coffee or tea will get your adventure gears turning. Tasty *and* revitalizing!

Don't Skimp on the SPF

Just because fire signs have a unique connection to the sun doesn't mean they still can't get burned by its power. Given the amount of time you spend outside keeping active, make sure to wear sunscreen and/or protect your skin with UV-blocking clothing. Hats are particularly important, as is reapplying sunscreen every hour or so when you are in the sun. If you've already spent too much time outside and gotten burned, a bottle of aloe vera gel can soothe the sting and help your skin heal more quickly.

Change Up Your Routine

Sagittarius loves trying new things—after all, if there is one thing he knows, it's that variety is truly the spice of life! It doesn't have to be some big adventure either. Is there a store you usually purchase your clothes from? Try out a different place this weekend. Is Thursday night out typically to the same local dive? Check out the new Italian restaurant in the next town over. Is there a go-to playlist you use when working out? Ask a friend or coworker with great musical taste to help you create a new mix.

Inspire Others

You are lucky to have such a powerful flame burning inside you. Fire signs may forget that not everyone possesses their same ambition and fervor. Use your natural fire for good and inspire someone else in your life.

Try sending a friend or a loved one a card of encouragement. The small gesture can help light a fire under them and give them the strength to take a risk. If sending a card isn't your cup of tea, a text, email, or phone call can offer the same sentiment. The goal is to reach out and share your own fire with someone else who needs it.

Let It Go

———————————

Holding on to negative emotions can do long-term damage to your well-being. Because of how passionate you can be as a fire sign, you may find you let resentment or other destructive feelings boil inside you. Let those feelings go. Don't allow them to fester and build inside of you until they get to an unmanageable point. Release any grudges you have against a person who has wronged you and forgive them for their wrongdoing. Once you let these emotions loose into the universe, you'll begin to heal and open up to more positivity and light.

Take a Risk

You already know that, as a fire sign, you have great instincts, but you may struggle with acting on them. Trust your gut and take a risk. Ask someone out on a date, apply for a new job, or make a large purchase that you've been eyeing for a while. Do something risky for yourself. It's easy to tell yourself "I'll do it later" or "It's not the right time." There's no time like the present. It might seem scary when you are in the moment, but big risks often mean big rewards. Tap into that passion churning inside you and take a leap of faith.

Nourish Your Spiritual Side

———————

Sagittarius seeks spiritual understanding, and historically he has been associated with positions in the clergy. Many influential clergy members were Sagittarians, including Pope Francis, Saint Junipero Serra, and Pope John XXIII (also known as the "Good Pope"). Feed your spiritual curiosities by reading a book on theology or philosophy. You can explore a traditional text such as the Bible, the Tanakh, or the works of Plato; or modern philosophical fables such as *The Alchemist* or *Life of Pi*.

Keep Moving Forward

This mantra, "Keep moving forward," is the spirit of Sagittarius. No matter what has occurred in the past, or what may be in store for the future, Sagittarius takes everything in stride, just like his intrepid astrology symbol, the Centaur. But, sometimes, a difficult day or situation can catch even the most confident and optimistic Sagittarius by surprise. Adopt this mantra, and repeat it to yourself whenever you are in need of a little boost of encouragement and reminder that no matter what obstacles may come your way, you have the strength and ingenuity to keep going forward.

Become a Gamer

Fire signs are competitive when it comes to just about anything. Even the most mundane of tasks can become a game for you, one that you just must win. To feed your competitive spirit in a healthy manner, try playing a board game. You're already used to being active outside, taking on one athletic challenge and then the next. Now train your mind. There are so many options to help you start flexing your brain muscles, from classic games like Monopoly and Scrabble to team games like charades, and even strategy and role-playing games. Buy a few and then have your friends over for a good old-fashioned game night!

Seek Your Fire Totem

Your fire is unique to you. To remind yourself of this, seek out a personal totem that symbolizes your fire and flame that you can keep with you at all times. A totem is a sacred object that serves as an emblem for a group of people. In your case this totem will symbolize your connection to the fire burning within. It could be a piece of jewelry such as a bracelet, necklace, cuff, or amulet, or even a small desk trinket that you can keep by your side at work. There's no right or wrong when it comes to choosing your totem. Focus on something that calls to you and makes you feel brave and powerful when it is in your presence.

Reclaim Your Dreams

———————

Part of the Native American tradition, dream catchers ward off bad dreams and promote deep, reflective sleep. Sagittarius has an affinity with all tribal cultures, appreciating their connection to nature and the spiritual realm. Always seeking spiritual growth, he also understands the intuitive language of dreams. Hang a dream catcher above your bed to keep the bad dreams away, so you can explore those deeper desires and obstacles in your subconscious. Seek out an authentic dream catcher made by a traditional craftsperson, and ask about the significance and history of this craft.

Make a Game of It

Fire signs can get bored easily. They are drawn to adventure and spontaneity, so the last thing they want is to get stuck in a pattern of tedium. Unfortunately, everyone has responsibilities they would rather not do, but how you react to those responsibilities is your choice. Tap into your fun-loving nature and make things more playful. Whether it's at work or around the house, turn your chores and responsibilities into a game. Even something as mundane as vacuuming the living room becomes a game when you set a timer for yourself. It makes things fun, feeds your competitive nature, and gets finished what needs to be done. In the end, changing how you think about a task can change how you complete it.

Smile

Smiling can change how you see the world, and how the world sees you. In fact some studies suggest that the physical act of smiling can trick your brain into being happy even when you are in a bad mood. As a fire sign, you have so much love and happiness inside you—let it shine through and catch on like wildfire. Make a deal with yourself to smile at one stranger a day. Because your happy energy is contagious as a fire sign, this small act of kindness could do wonders for boosting someone's mood.

Treat Yourself

———————————

You spend a lot of time entertaining those around you. The energy you have as a fire sign is infectious, so it's no wonder that people are drawn to you. You also love making people smile and laugh—it comes naturally and boosts your mood. Despite your penchant for entertaining, it's important to give yourself a break every once in a while. Alone time can be just as beneficial as time spent with large groups. Take yourself out to dinner once a month as a treat. To keep things lively, sit at the bar and people-watch. Keep yourself open to new conversation with other bar patrons. Allowing your server to wait on you for once will help rejuvenate your spirit.

Promote Overall Health with Reflexology

Sagittarius is always on his feet. Reflexology is an alternative therapy that involves applying pressure to certain areas on your feet with specific finger and thumb techniques. Depending on where and how reflexologists apply the pressure, they can aim to reduce stress, improve a headache, promote proper liver and kidney function, and more. Many physical therapy locations offer reflexology massages, and you can also find more information and "foot maps" online to try your own hand at reflexology.

Try a Fire Craft

Fuel your creative spark by taking up a craft that is powered by fire. While regular crafting such as painting, drawing, and sculpting are all wonderful ways to unwind and explore your artistic side, as a fire sign you crave something with a little more heat. Try pottery making, glassblowing, or woodburning to satiate your appetite. Your innate connection to fire will only deepen your creative reach and encourage your imagination. Find inspiration in how the heat transforms different materials—how it hardens clay, melts glass, and singes wood. Honor the power of fire through the creative process.

Top Your Toast with Lingonberry Jam

Bright, sweet lingonberries are ruled by Jupiter, and both the Native American history and medicinal properties of the berry will delight Sagittarius. Some traditional Native American cultures use the berries or juice to ease colds and sore throats, and in folk medicine they are believed to treat nerve issues. Just like Jupiter these berries are colorful orbs of vitality, promoting a healthy Sagittarius. Look for lingonberry jam in stores, and spread it over your morning toast, or use it to make thumbprint cookies with a twist when you are in need of a sweet treat.

Binge a New Show

––––––––––

There's nothing quite like snuggling up on the couch in front of your TV (or laptop) after a long day. As a fire sign you've probably been jumping from one activity to the next, trying to keep active and keep yourself moving. But there's nothing wrong with slowing down for a bit. Binge-watching a new show can be the perfect break you need from your hectic schedule. Make a night of it, and burn through every episode you can find. Make a bowl of popcorn, open a bottle of wine, and kick off your shoes. Let yourself become obsessed with knowing what happens next.

Become More Patient

Fire signs have so many wonderful personality traits. Your level of loyalty, ambition, and passion is something to be envied. But you also have some unfavorable traits that you can work on. For example, your fieriness can often be interpreted by others as impatience. As a fire sign your emotions tend to escalate very quickly, and your intensity can sometimes get the best of you.

Patience is a skill that often takes practice. Make it a personal goal to become more patient with others, situations, and yourself. When you feel that you are losing your patience, take a few deep breaths to de-escalate your emotions before they go too far. You have the power to control how you react to what you are feeling inside.

Start an Idea Book

Fire signs are known for their creativity and great ideas. Don't risk letting those good ideas slip away by not taking the time to write them down. Consider buying an idea journal where you can keep track of all the cool things that you come up with on a daily basis. Similar to a dream journal, an idea journal is the perfect place to house your million-dollar thoughts. These journals are specifically created to help you tease out and capture your next great idea, and many even have prompts to inspire and challenge you. Never forget another genius idea again!

Fight for Your Rights

U se your passion to change the world. Fire signs have a lot of strong opinions and personal beliefs. Identify those causes that mean the most to you and put all of your energy into fighting for them. Whether it's environmental issues, animal welfare, women's and LGBTQ+ rights, veterans' affairs, or anything else that lights your fire, know that you can make a difference just by showing up and being present. Start by joining a social media group that gives updates about organized protests near you. Volunteer on weekends at local shelters. Make signs for rallies. Whatever it takes. Fight for what you believe, and inspire and motivate others to do the same.

Use a Standing Desk

Sagittarius is an active sign that can experience back pain or other muscle tension when sitting still for too long. After all, your muscles were made for adventure! Use a standing desk (or ball chair, if standing isn't an option) to keep your spine straight and avoid these physical aches. The frequent movement will also keep you feeling refreshed and focused on the task at hand so you can get things done with ease. Many companies have inexpensive desk attachments to raise your computer or surface work space to whatever level is best for you.

Try a Rose Mist

S elf-care may not come easy to a fire sign. You are used to caring for others, and can sometimes forget to tend your own fire. Before you know it, your flame is burning out of control. A refreshing mist is a quick and easy way to balance the fire inside you, and to give yourself a few moments of self-care that you otherwise may pass up.

Rosewater is especially therapeutic for irritated skin. Rosewater is a hydrating blend made by steeping rose petals in water. Spritz it over clean skin and breathe in the calming scent of roses.

While you can find rosewater in many grocery and health stores, you can also make your own. First, find an empty spray bottle. Next, boil a large pot of water, and remove the petals from a few roses. Add the petals to the water, and allow to simmer over medium-high heat for 20–30 minutes until the petals have lost the majority of their color. Allow to cool, strain the petals, and add the water to your spray bottle.

Stretch

Sagittarius rules the thighs and also the legs. Be sure to stretch these muscles well before exercising to avoid strain—you'll need them strong for your next adventure! Great stretches that target the thigh and leg muscle groups include the hamstring stretch and the standing quadriceps stretch.

To do the hamstring stretch, stand straight and bend over, coming as close as you can to touching your toes without bending your knees. Hold for 5 seconds, then stand up straight, and repeat the stretch once or twice more.

To do the standing quadriceps stretch, stand straight and bend one leg back, grabbing your ankle with one hand. Bend your knee back as far as possible and hold for 30 seconds. Repeat with your other leg.

Find Joy in "Ode to Joy"

Playful and optimistic, there is no sign better suited for such a celebration of joy than Sagittarius. In fact, Sagittarian Beethoven's "Ode to Joy" should be the Sagittarius theme song. However, even the vivacious Sagittarius experiences a few bumps in the road that can make remaining positive a bit more challenging. Keep this song on your phone and hit the play button whenever you need a little reminder of the things that make you—and the world around you— so amazing.

Have a Solo Dance Party

B reak out your dancing shoes and turn on your favorite jam. It's time for a solo dance party! Dancing is a wonderful way for fire signs to expel built-up energy that they haven't been able to let go of yet. It gets your heart pumping and your endorphins flowing. Plus, it's just plain fun. Let loose and really go for it. There's no one there to judge your dance moves or the song you pick to boogie down to. Let the music take control and just go with it. Feel like doing the electric slide? Do it. Want to practice your running man? There's no time like the present!

Take Your Vitamins

Your body is a temple, and it needs the proper nourishment to stay strong and healthy. Fire signs are constantly pushing their physical limits by taking on new athletic challenges. To keep your body from getting run-down, it's important to stick to a vitamin regimen every day. Talk to your doctor about which vitamins are best for you. There are even companies that offer personalized vitamin packs based on your individual needs. Even just a simple multivitamin made for your age group or gender can give your body the boost it needs.

Stargaze

The universe is expansive. Just look up at the sky on a pitch-black night. There are tiny suns and balls of flaming gas millions of miles away. Some estimates suggest there are approximately one hundred billion stars in just the Milky Way alone. Imagine how many more there are in the billions of other galaxies in the universe.

Your presence in this universe is important. Never lose the passion and heat you have burning inside you as a fire sign. It can be easy to feel small sometimes. When you are feeling lost, look up at the stars. They can help you find your way. And if you are lucky, you may even discover the constellations of one of the fire signs—Aries, Leo, or Sagittarius—to guide you.

Enjoy a Mai Tai Punch

This tropical treat captures the Sagittarius sense of adventure. All you will need are 1½ ounces spiced rum, 1½ ounces coconut-flavored rum, 1 teaspoon grenadine syrup, 3 ounces pineapple juice, 2 ounces orange juice, 1 cup ice cubes, and 1 maraschino cherry. In a cocktail mixer filled with ice, combine the spiced rum, coconut rum, grenadine, pineapple juice, and orange juice. Shake and strain into a rocks glass filled with fresh ice. Top with the cherry and a festive drink umbrella or two.

Burn Cedarwood Oil

Robust cedar invokes the smell of nature—perfect for the outdoorsy Sagittarius. If you've been cooped up inside due to a cold or disagreeable weather, the aroma of cedar will transport you to the lush forests and towering mountains that you have been missing.

To burn the essential oil, simply place it in water in the shallow bowl of an oil burner, and then place a lit tea light in the chamber underneath. Don't have an oil burner? You can also use it in a mist diffuser. Cedarwood oil is an organic insect repellent that you can bring on your adventures to ward off pesky mosquitoes without releasing harmful chemicals into the air or onto your skin. Rubbing the oil (diluted according to package instructions) into your scalp is also said to promote a healthy mane.

Find the Funny

Ruled by jovial Jupiter, Sagittarius exults in laughter and the friendly practical joke. Sometimes life can get a bit overwhelming—even for optimistic Sagittarius—and finding the whimsy in a situation is more of a challenge. Feed your inner comedian by watching a funny video on your phone, playing a joke on a good friend, or listening to a comedy podcast on your way to work in the morning. Taking the time to delight in something humorous every day will keep your positivity stores brimming.

Pause with Purple Jade

Sometimes Sagittarius can get a bit enthusiastic, and the words tumble out before he has a chance to think them over. Carry a purple jade stone to encourage taking that much-needed pause before saying what is on your mind.

Purple jade taps into your connection with the world and people around you by opening your crown chakra, which controls how you perceive and react to your surroundings. Carrying this stone with you will encourage well-thought-out responses to every situation.

Travel Through Your
Taste Buds

A favorite spice in Mexican and Indian cuisine (and also a signature Sagittarian flavor), anise will jump-start Sagittarius's energy, while taking him on a one-way trip to the bustling streets and luminescent shoreline of Mumbai.

For the full exotic experience whenever your wanderlust emerges, make an easy curry powder to season soups, rice, sauces, and more. Simply toast 1 tablespoon whole anise seeds, 2 tablespoons whole coriander seeds, 1 tablespoon whole cumin seeds, 1 tablespoon whole mustard seeds, 1½ teaspoons whole fenugreek seeds, and 1½ teaspoons whole all-spice berries in a pan until very fragrant. Grind the toasted seeds together, toss in 2 tablespoons turmeric powder, and store in a sealed container until ready to use.

Visit a Body of Water

Warm and energetic, Sagittarius is a fiery sign with places to be. A little soothing water will balance your fire and allow you to relax and recharge your batteries before an excursion. You can take a walk along a river, meditate on a lake or beach shore, or break out your inflatable recliner and float in the pool. Whichever watery experience you choose, be sure to focus your full attention on it. Feel yourself connecting to the water through your senses, and breathe deeply as you walk, meditate, or float.

Detox with Clove Essential Oil

I t is claimed that clove essential oil protects the liver, which is also governed by Sagittarius. The liver flushes out the toxins that can lead to many health problems, so a healthy liver is crucial to a healthy you. Being a spice, clove is also the perfect essential oil for fiery Sagittarius. Clove also prevents the inflammation that may occur when you are out trying all of those exotic foods during your travels. Sparingly rub the (diluted according to instructions) oil onto your skin or diffuse it to aid detoxification and other benefits.

Honor Commitments

Make a commitment to honoring commitments! Sagittarius gallops through life, with so many things to do and so much energy behind each step. Keeping track of every promise and every important date can be tricky in all of the excitement of your upcoming plans. Whether promises are romantic, work, social, or family oriented, staying true to your promises is essential in respecting both your time and the time of others. Keep a calendar, set phone reminders, and implore friends and family to work with you to ensure that you uphold your commitments.

Go for a Hike

———————

Get out and get moving in nature. A hike through a nearby forest or mountain trail is the perfect combination of the Sagittarian love of adventure and love of the great outdoors. Savor the lush, organic colors, sounds of birds or other critters, and earthy smells you encounter on your hike. Once you've had the chance to get some sun and physical activity, and to delight in Mother Nature's beauty, you'll feel renewed and fully recharged for whatever may lie ahead.

Watch a Documentary

Sagittarius loves to learn—and a fun, informative documentary is the perfect way to learn something new while relaxing, or staying dry on a rainy day. Always searching for spiritual enlightenment and the secrets of the intangible world, Sagittarius will enjoy documentaries on different religions and experiences with the metaphysical. UFO sightings, documented encounters with spirits, and accounts of miraculous healing will all catch his eye.

You can also experience the great outdoors—even when the weather outside your window is less than ideal—with a nature documentary. Learn about the intelligence and social habits of different animal species.

Revisit an Unfinished Project

Sagittarius is full of exciting ideas and has ample energy to hit the ground running. However, sometimes in his enthusiasm for finding the "next big thing," he can get caught up in a new project before finishing the previous one. When you find yourself on the lookout for a new venture, ask yourself, "Is there a project I have started in the past but haven't yet completed?" Once you pinpoint an unfinished project, you can come up with a revitalized plan to see it through to completion.

Savor Your Mornings

———————

Wake up a little earlier than necessary so you have time to really enjoy the quiet hours before work or your weekend plans. Plan out your to-do list for the day, go for a jog around the neighborhood, or perhaps meditate with a cup of coffee. Embrace the day! A morning ritual is the perfect way to charge your batteries and head out the door rejuvenated and ready for whatever you have in store.

Watch Out for Jupiter

———————————

Jupiter, the ruling planet over Sagittarius, represents knowledge, justice, prosperity, optimism, and personal growth. Be mindful of where your celestial ruler is currently positioned: when it will be visible from your location, which planets it will be aligned with when, and on what dates it will transit the sun. Your natal chart can provide more details on what each position means for you, and which positions will affect your life the most (these will be the ones to be especially mindful of).

Go to a Museum

Sagittarius loves to explore and learn new things. A trip to a local museum allows you to get the best of both—at little to no cost. Check out how different parts of the body work at a science museum, discover amazing species that once roamed the earth in a natural history museum, or fall in love with a moving exhibit at an art museum. Of course you can tap into your Sagittarian sense of adventurous even more with a trip to a famous national or even international museum if you please!

Take Time for Yourself

Restore your shining Sagittarius spirit with a bit of alone time. Sagittarius is used to being the leader of the pack, but a little space to relax and reflect can be just the thing he needs to return to the task or excursion at hand with a rejuvenated sense of enthusiasm and energy. Take an hour, afternoon, or day to relax alone in whichever way you prefer, whether it be a bubble bath, a good book, or even a run through a local nature trail (sometimes exercising is just as relaxing to Sagittarius as a nap on the couch is to others!).

Subscribe to a Podcast

Sagittarius loves to learn—and stay on the move. A podcast allows you to do both with a quick, often free, subscription. With the big wide world at your fingertips thanks to ever-advancing technology, you can find an overwhelming range of podcasts on a variety of topics, so you can choose just what excites you. The philosopher and theologian Sagittarius will love topics such as ethics, the teachings of Socrates, personal experiences with spirituality, and different spiritual beliefs. Download podcasts that catch your eye and listen to them during car rides, while out for a run, or in your downtime.

Take a Quick Work Break

Hardworking and brimming with energy and enthusiasm, Sagittarius is often known at work as the one who is always going, going, going. Make sure to take a break every once in a while to refocus and reenergize when you feel stuck on a project or feel like you could use a nap. Go for a walk outside if the weather is nice, run an easy errand, or sip a tea or coffee at a local coffee shop. Step away from your desk for 10 minutes—even when it may seem counterproductive—and you'll be surprised by how rejuvenated you feel when you return to work.

Practice Honesty
with Yourself

Sagittarius prides himself on being honest. While honesty with others comes naturally, being honest with yourself can be a bit more challenging, whether it is to celebrate the things that make you great or acknowledge the things that you can work on. Practice being more honest with yourself. Take the time to pay yourself compliments while also looking into the things you can improve. It may help to write things down so you can further explore these truths, and also return to them when you are in need of a refresher.

Encourage Healthy Liver Function with Berries

Sagittarius rules over the liver, which flushes your body of toxins and stores iron and a number of important vitamins. Blueberries and cranberries are full of liver-promoting properties, including antioxidants like anthocyanin, which also gives them their striking colors. They are also delicious sources of vitamin C, and may inhibit tumor growth.

You can make a simple jam with the berries to top your morning toast, give the traditional PB&J (peanut butter and jelly) sandwich a twist, stir into plain yogurt, or pour over meat. Just simmer cranberries from one 12-ounce package and ½ cup sugar in 1 cup water for 10 minutes, then mash slightly. Stir in 1 teaspoon cinnamon, ¼ teaspoon nutmeg, and ⅛ teaspoon ground allspice, then remove from heat and add 16 ounces of blueberries. Enjoy!

About the Author

Constance Stellas is an astrologer of Greek heritage with more than twenty-five years of experience. She primarily practices in New York City and counsels a variety of clients, including business CEOs, artists, and scholars. She has been interviewed by *The New York Times*, *Marie Claire*, and *Working Woman*, and has appeared on several New York TV morning shows, featuring regularly on Sirius XM and other national radio programs as well. Constance is the astrologer for *HuffPost* and a regular contributor to Thrive Global. She is also the author of several titles, including *The Astrology Gift Guide*, *Advanced Astrology for Life*, *The Everything® Sex Signs Book*, and the graphic novel series Tree of Keys, as well as coauthor of *The Hidden Power of Everyday Things*. Learn more about Constance at her website, ConstanceStellas.com, or on *Twitter* (@Stellastarguide).

Create a Personal Altar

Sagittarius is deeply connected to spirituality. Create a personal altar that is unique to you and your own spirituality. As a fiery zodiac sign, you can burn a candle on a pedestal that is a cool, water-inspired color such as blue or deep purple to promote balance, or create a space on a mantelpiece, if you have one, to decorate with small objects that motivate and uplift you. These objects can include photographs, elements of nature, and an oil diffuser with your favorite scents.